THINK BIG

START SMALL

SCALE FAST!

STORIES FROM THE STAGE
ON INNOVATION, DISRUPTION
AND THE ACCELERATING FUTURE

FUTURIST JIM CARROLL

OBLIO Press, www.obliopress.com

Carroll, Jim, 1959-
        Think Big, Start Small, Scale Fast / Jim Carroll

ISBN 978-0-9736554-7-6

Production Credits:
Editor: Christa Carroll
Photo Editor: Willie Carroll
Cover Design: Willie Carroll

Table of Contents

To Christa, Willie & Thomas

In the complexity that is my mind and the unfocused manner by which I float through the day, know that there is undying love inside me each and every day.

To all of my friends in a 'new life' journey

Turning the future into opportunity is all about knowing the opportunities that you can pursue, the challenges you should avoid, and making the right decision each and every day. You might never have known it, but I was always listening carefully to what you were saying. Somehow, your words and observations inspired one of the daily quotes that became a key part of my journey.

Introduction

How did this book come about? What does it actually cover? It is a story of inspiration, observation and transformation.

I've been speaking to organizations around the world for well over 25 years about the future and the attitudes and actions that can help us to turn it into a world of opportunity.

Somewhere along the way, I came to realize that this unique experience, a life on the stage, had provided me with some very unique insights into how people try to deal with a world of massive change and challenge.

In late July 2016, through a variety of colliding circumstances, the opportunity to focus my thinking into a message of hope and inspiration took on a life of its own. Since that moment in time, I have started each and every workday, without fail, very early in the morning, with my coffee, my laptop, and a moment of quiet reflection. They are a critical part of a very important journey, that of painting a picture of hope and optimism each and every day for what the day might bring. These observations - usually inspirational, sometimes controversial - are layered on top of a photo where I had appeared on stage and then shared with people via my social networks.

How important are they? I have not missed one day since starting this in early August 2016. I mark my personal progress and success one day at a time by my ability to inspire myself and others each and every day through this small personal thought.

This book captures but a small number of those morning reflections. As of this writing, I am approaching close to 1,000. You can find all of them at https://inspiration.jimcarroll.com

I am forever grateful for the opportunity to inspire people worldwide.

Infinite Possibilities!

"The possibilities are infinte
when you start out with nothing!"

In many situations, low points define the highest points of opportunity for people.

We've all been there at some time or another — hitting a point that is challenging, without a lot of hope, where success seems elusive, perhaps hitting a point of emotional and spiritual collapse. Life is full of those ups and downs — it's a part of the deal.

The Story Behind the Picture

My own career went down a path that at one time seemed hopeless.

In 1988, my company was merging; my future path was cut off; no one understood the potential of this 'stupid' thing that was to become the internet. I was told I should be like other people and follow a traditional career path.

And yet, I was convinced that something huge was about to happen with the marriage of technology and connectivity.

So I quit my job, left my career, and with the help of my wife, started doing my own thing. I wrote a bunch of books, hosted radio shows, had newspaper columns and other writing opportunities turning my obsession with technology into a wonderful career.

Today, I travel the world, advising people on how to take advantage of the next infinite possibilities that can come about.

And yet, when you are at that point, you might have the chance to realize that the opportunities in front of you are wide open, if only you commit!

It's when you have nothing that you have the opportunity for everything. If you focus and take the future one day at a time, you will have endless opportunity through renewal.

Surround yourself with people who think like you — those who will help you realize there is a pathway out, and that a road less travelled can help turn things around in a magical, wonderful, life-defining manner!

There Is A Child Alive

"There is a child alive today who will jump into a flying car at some point in their lifetime, it will quickly whiz them to their destination on its own."

The future will happen — but eventually!

That's a good mindset to deal with the reality that when it comes to the future, the big challenge is not necessarily knowing what the trends are, it's increasingly, when are they going to happen?

We might have any number of trends which will impact an industry going forward — artificial intelligence, blockchain, disintermediation, the acceleration of customer expectations, the emergence of new competitors, and more. Yet, when might any of these trends become real and have a significant, disruptive impact?

11

The Story Behind the Photo

The photo is from a U.K. private client meeting for a group of senior executives of a major financial services firm. They are in the insurance, commercial and personal banking industries.

They brought me in to challenge their thinking on the future and what they might start doing to align themselves to the fast trends of today. I spoke about the issue of self-driving electric cars and presented the challenges that come with such a massive industry shift.

Such as, what happens to the auto lending process when a 21 year old today expects to be able to get approval for an auto loan in 45 seconds or less on their mobile device? How do we sell automative insurance in an era in which many people have stopped buying cars because of the rise of car sharing services and in which the number of automative incidents decreases because of intelligent highway technology?

How will they actually come about, and when? That can be a bigger issue than the actual trend itself.

I'll grant that the road to the future is often difficult, complex and challenging to manage, but the impact of any trend in the long run is real.

So it is with the concept of a flying car — one day, we will live in a world in which they are common. Today, they are but a science fiction curiosity. Somewhere between today and tomorrow, a lot has to happen to make them real.

The best you can do is to make sure you are ready with your strategy, have built up your experience, and have the flexibility to move fast when it happens.

In other words — think big, start small, scale fast!

Accelerate Your Imaginuity

"Stuck in a rut?
Accelerate your imaginuity!"

I n Wisconsin, there is a store that goes by the name Imaginuity. Their tag line? "Play with a purpose!" They've nailed the concept right there!

So to is the concept of "imaginuity," it's a combination of "imagination" and "creativity", and is the perfect blend of the concept of ideas and creativity.

When I came across the word I realized that I've really been speaking on stage about the concept of 'imaginuity' for years.

The Story Behind the Picture

Last week, someone questioned my use of the word "imaginating" in my daily quote, noting that it 'isn't a word.' And so one morning, I coined an entirely new word based on the concept of 'imaginating.'

The actual photo is from a keynote I did for the National Coffee, Tea & Water Association Annual Conference. One of their key issues was how to keep up with the new competitors entering their industry at a fast clip, with unique new branding messages, effective social media campaigns, and a high degree of effectiveness with short attention span millennials. A part of my keynote spoke about new trends in branding and marketing, and the need to continually explore all the radical new ideas surrounding them — and then challenge their old traditional thinking. Not necessarily imaginuity, but certainly creative thinking!

I'm big on the power of the imagination, so much so that years ago, I suggested that some universities should start offering a degree known as the "Masters in Business Imagination!" No one took me up on it, I guess most are stifled by their lack of creativity!

What will give you a great sense of imaginuity? First and foremost, imagine the impossible. That's the real essence of innovative thinking — you need to think of things that are not possible, things not yet made, or ideas not yet pursued. All of the great inventions of our time have relied upon the power of someone's imagination.

Turn the ideas into reality through creative thinking. How do you do that? Innovative organizations accelerate their creativity by turning their innovation engines upside down, focusing on customer oriented innovation and other unique new innovation models. They excel at sourcing ideas from the outside through the unique innovations occurring within crowdsourcing and crowdfunding sites, turning that unique insight into fuel for their internal innovation factories. They challenge themselves on speed by getting into an iterative process of constantly rethinking, adjusting and redoing in order to discover the next best thing. They explore the boundaries of the new methods of thinking and innovating on a continuous basis.

Failure? It's An Attitude

"Failure?
It's an attitude that precedes its actual occurrence!"

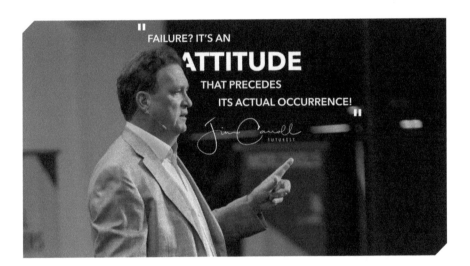

Your mindset determines your success — that's always been true.

And so if you set out with the idea of failure in your mind, guess what — you are likely to fail! If you think you'll have a marginal performance, you probably will. If you convince yourself you won't be able to — you won't be able to.

But if you put your mind into a mode in which you are thinking about success, chances are you might be able to pull it off. And if you don't? You've given it a pretty good shot and you'll try again because you touched the edges of success.

The Story Behind the Picture

This one is from Sao Paolo, Brazil. I was there to headline the Global Worldskills Conference. It's an initiative designed to encourage young people to pursue careers and opportunities in skilled trades.

And it's actually sort of like a mini-Olympics for those trades. Individuals aged 17 to 21 from over 85 countries compete in challenges related to plumbing, electrical, welding or other traditional skills, in addition to advanced careers in computer aided design, aircraft maintenance and other trades.

With that, the mindset of many of the young people participating from around the world was similar to that of a traditional Olympian — "failure is not an option!"

Study the history of the greatest innovative minds of our time, and you'll find people who are relentlessly focused on success. Or in other cases, you'll find others who have had failure in mind, but didn't really view the failure as, well, a failure: "I have not failed once. I've just found 10,000 ways that didn't work." -- Thomas Edison. Think about the context of that remark — he didn't really fail in the traditional way. Instead, it was a building block for success.

The same holds true for James Dyson, who invented the Dyson vacuum. He actually spent 15 years with some 5,127 prototypes that didn't quite work before bringing a successful product to market in 1993. He also viewed failure in a different way: "Stumbling upon the next great invention in an "ah-hah!" moment is a myth. It is only by learning from mistakes that progress is made...each failure brought me closer to solving a problem."

So on this Monday, start out your week with the idea of success firmly embedded in your mind — or think about potential failure not as failure, but as a stepping stone to eventual success!

Get Ahead!

"Get ahead of the fast future,
before it gets ahead of you!"

see a lot of organizations and people fall behind trends which are often blindingly obvious. The challenge, of course, is that in their day to day activities, they aren't charged with the responsibility for watching carefully what comes next, and what they should do about it. The result is that they wake up one day, take a look around, and realize that suddenly, everything has changed.

Obviously, not a good way to be!

The Story Behind the Picture

The picture is from a keynote I did for an organization in London, England — a leading global food company.

The focus of my keynote was on fast-paced consumer trends in the world of retail, the shopping experience, consumer behaviour, how brands interact with consumers in an era of declining attention spans, the impact of intelligent packaging and a wide variety of other trends.

This type of event is typical of many that I do. All kinds of organizations bring me in for up to date insight on the key trends that are or will impact them going forward, in order that they can align their activities to the future. I help them to understand the challenges and opportunities of these trends, and a path forward in terms of innovation around these trends.

I will often wrap up these talks with specific guidance that will help their senior executives do what is necessary for that alignment. The thought process behind this quote is often one that I will use — in that I'll speak about the importance of having a good 'trends radar.'

"Trends radar" is a concept I first outlined on stage in the 1990's, and which made its way into my book, *What I Learned from Frogs in Texas.* In that book, I wrote:

> Innovation comes from the ability to see the obvious, and so the first step in the loop is to establish a form of "trends radar" that keeps you attuned to the future.

> Everyone throughout the organization should be prepared to keep a constant eye out for new developments and opportunities that might impact your business or market, and that might provide opportunity for innovation. They should also be watching for trends, issues or signs that might indicate a potential threat or looming challenge.

> Each of them has an understanding that having good radar can help the organization spot future opportunities and act upon them, as well as do what is necessary to ward off and deal with potential threats.

I am a big believer that every individual, and every organization should establish their own specialized form of an effective trends radar. Regardless of what we are responsible for day-to-day, we should have the ability to track and understand the major trends that will impact our operations, competitors, skills issues and much more.

And even more important — what are we doing to share what we see so that we can effectively respond?

So ask yourself the question today: do you have an effective trends radar?

If not, develop one!

Antidote For Velocity!

"Agility is the only antidote for velocity"

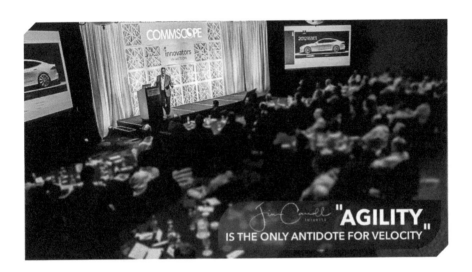

One recent client engaged me for a talk for their global team, with the keynote title *"Achieving Agility: Aligning Ourselves for an Era of Accelerating Change"*. That's a good example of how I outline the attributes for success in a world of high velocity change. With that, I focused on how organizations and leaders must incorporate four key capabilities: agility, insight, innovation and execution.

The Story Behind the Picture

This particular photo is from a keynote for a high tech company customer conference. Their clients are in data communications, server and networking industries — both cloud companies as well as corporate organizations.

In that industry, the ability to move and respond quickly in terms of the infrastructure to support the business is becoming paramount because of the rapid emergence of new technologies and methodologies. Tech is being inundated with new stuff: the Internet of Things, cloud computing, robotics and much more. Fast technology leads to disruption, changes in business models, the emergence of new competitors and rapidly changing customer expectations.

Organizations are having to scramble in terms of strategies, skills and structure. My story on stage that day was how we need to accelerate our technology deployment in order to support those changes.

Agile is a concept that originally developed in the world of software development, but has recently taken on greater meaning as an overall management framework. It is what it implies: the ability to work and deliver faster, not by concentrating on one large scale project with a final deliverable, but through an iterative process of small scale steps, each of which can be fixed at any particular time.

Agile structure is critical given fast industry change. Consider the world of retail, specifically: the rapid emergence of new forms of in-store promotion known as "shopper marketing," which combines location intelligence, mobile technology and in-store display technology; massive changes to the in-store payment process, including mobile payment involving Apple Pay and the complete elimination of the concept of the cash-register; the emergence of same-day shipping from titans such as Google, Amazon and Walmart; the rapid installation of "click and collect" infrastructure (i.e. an online purchase, with same day pickup at a retail location); faster 'store fashion' with rapid evolution of in-store promotion, layout and interaction; the arrival of intelligent packaging and intelligent ("Internet of Things") products; and collapsing product life-cycles, rapid product obsolescence and the implications on inventory and supply chain! Not to mention all the fast changing consumer, taste, food and social networking trends influencing today's food purchasing decisions.

How do you achieve agility in a fast moving environment?

◆ structure for execution

◆ rebuild your competitive intelligence capabilities

- watch the "edges", particular crowdfunding initiatives in your space
- abandon tradition — get more projects on the leading edge
- be decisive — avoid aggressive indecision
- innovate with structure — form fast teams!
- encourage entrepreneurial units — spin out units rather than reining them in
- partner up in unique ways
- redefine strategic planning — flex it to short term thinking
- build a culture that supports new ideas
- challenge decisions
- rapidly ingest new technology
- "test and learn"
- spot trends quicker
- risk failure faster
- align different generations on social projects.

Agility implies that we must innovate and adapt based on rapidly changing circumstances, on a continuous basis.

Starting Line

"If you are going to show up at the starting line for the future, make sure that you don't show up late!"

One of my key responsibilities as a futurist is to help my clients, some of the largest associations and companies in the world, align themselves to the fast paced trends of today.

One key question that always comes up? "When do we get involved with any key trend?"

I walk them through that issue from a variety of perspectives and with observations I've seen from spending time with countless Fortune 1000 organizations. However, I stress that when it comes to the issue of timing, it is critical that they get involved in some way with any new trend or technology.

The Story Behind the Picture

I'm on stage in Boston, speaking to the annual conference of the Powder Metal Manufacturing Association. Fast trends are having a huge impact on this industry — particularly 3D printing and the arrival of the new business models related to that.

They are having to innovate faster in terms of discovery and development of new materials, as well as work hard to line themselves up to the new players in the additive manufacturing marketplace. Since many of them are of a relatively small or medium size, hesitation in action can be their middle name — they are like many other industries, in that it is easier to postpone necessary action rather than taking it on.

Some don't and as a result, their inaction and indecision end up costing them dearly!

History has taught us that when it comes to key trends, some organizations don't bother showing up at all or don't show up at the right time — and end up missing a lot of opportunities. Hence, the quote in the picture!

How do you determine when to invest? The best guidance comes from something called the "Gartner Hypecycle."

Years ago, the global research company suggested that any new technology goes along a curve — it appears, hits the time of excessive hype and expectations, that is followed by the inevitable collapse of enthusiasm as people realize that it takes a lot of time and effort to implement the technology and determine the opportunity that comes from it. But inevitably, both the expectations and technology itself mature and it becomes a key component for innovation and so much more.

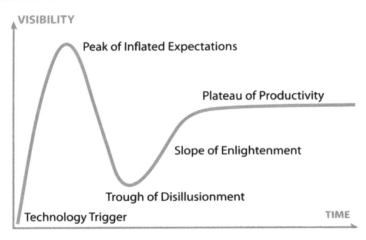

You can take any technology and place it on the curve.

Consider e-commerce: it appeared, and people got carried away with the potential during the dot.com era of the late 1990's. However, that involved a period of rather excessive and ridiculous hype, and so we had the inevitable dot.com collapse. Plateau of productivity?

Amazon is steamrolling retail in North America, and Alibaba dominates retail trends in China. Everywhere, stores are closing and online shopping is accelerating. Amazon buys Whole Foods. Do you get the point?

Now consider the explosion of new technologies around us today: 3D printing, the Internet of Things (#IoT), virtual reality, artificial intelligence, self-driving cars. A key component to your strategy is figuring out where they are on the curve, and hence, what you should be doing with them in terms of an innovation strategy. There are some useful observations to be found online which takes the hypecycle and places a variety of technologies at their current point on the curve.

But here's the thing: if a key technology shows an opportunity, don't ignore it if it is still early days otherwise there is a good chance that you won't be ready when it becomes real — when it hits the plateau of productivity.

This is where my "think big, start small, scale fast" mantra comes into play. Even if it is early days, you should make sure that you are working with, experimenting with, and gaining expertise in any new technology. Fail early and fail fast! That way, you will be better positioned when it hits the "plateau of productivity."

One thing I've learned? Some organizations don't take this step. They don't show up to the starting line! They are too dismissive of new ideas and new technologies. The result is that they don't even appear in the race, and miss out on building up the early expertise and experience with a key technology.

It's Inevitable

"What part of 'it's inevitable'
did you not understand?

People are aware of many disruptive trends, but then go into denial as to their likelihood of happening. I see it all the time.

Then they complain when the future happens!

Perhaps, deep inside, they are wishing for some relief from change; they silently hope that time stands still; that progress won't march on.

Yet the future doesn't hold back. It's relentless, unstoppable, a force of nature as inviolable as mass, gravity and light. Why fight the reality of what it represents?

The Story Behind the Picture

I'm on stage in Las Vegas, an opening keynote for the American Fire Protection Association. It's a group that represents the firefighting and fire safety industry.

It was a very unique trends talk that I pulled together on several unique themes — the acceleration of new forms of fire risk, for example. Everything from home hoarding (which presents new problems as different forms of hoarding present different forms of fire fighting strategy!) to the impact of solar infrastructure on aerial sprayer deployment (it's more complicated) to hot fires from electric vehicle batteries.

But I also touched on the inevitability of various trends in the industry — the arrival of autonomous, aerial firefighting drones, for example. Certain trends are inevitable, and my message was that it is important to be aligned to them.

But people do, and the consequences become all too harsh — business models disappear, products become obsolete, brand propositions blow up, new competitors steamroll the old structure; other nations innovate while you stand still.

Inevitability should drive many of your decisions and actions. Otherwise, you'll spend more time looking back with regret, and less time looking forward for opportunity!

Imaginate More!

"Imaginate more! Sweat the 'big stuff' - don't get distracted by the details!"

Of course, "imaginate" is not officially a word, but it should be! With that, the Urban Dictionary, which does a great job in finding and documenting new emerging words, actually defines 'imaginate' this way: "To be in the process of imagining, to form a mental picture of, to think, or believe. i.e. sometimes when in class Jesse imaginates and doesn't finish his work."

The Story Behind the Picture

Imaginate. That would be me! I think I finally found the word that defines me! My family would probably agree.

"Sometimes when dad is around the house he's busy imaginating and doesn't help with cleaning up."

Yup.

A busy mind is not something you want to waste — try and find a balance between participating in the world around you while you are busy thinking about the next one!

And maybe, that's you! Do you imagine enough? If not, why not?

To imagine our future and be relentlessly innovative, you need to take your mind into a different creative space. Don't be distracted by those around you who will say 'it can't be done,' 'how will you make it work,' or 'there are too many potential problems with your idea.' Those are the details that will immediately shut down your imaginating machine.

The fact is, there are people around you who will try to put up barriers, lay down guardrails, and implement cages for your mind. Break free! Escape the shackles of their limitations and imagine what might come next! Make sure to take time to imaginate, because you can't always unplug. Carve out some free time or 'play time' to explore the world around you.

Behind the scenes, I'm a hard core computer geek and have been since 1982. I'm always playing with new technology — Raspberry Pi's, Linux systems, IoT devices, networking stuff and tech toys. It helps me to understand what it is people are really talking about when they are inventing the future all around me.

Sweat the big stuff, not the small things!

Dream big, think big, imagine your world in a big way.

It's one of the best ways to understand what comes next.

Creative Energy

"To really accelerate your creative energy, focus on growing your diversity of ideas"

For years, I've explained to my global client base that access to new external skills and talent will be the key element for success going forward. Two good examples? Fast trends in the world of self-driving cars and the acceleration of trends in retail.

The Story Behind the Picture

I'm on stage opening the annual meeting of the National Recreation and Parks Association, with a few thousand individuals from the industry in the room. I was telling the story of the rapid emergence of Zorbing, and the idea of 'Pac-Man in the streets'. Both were new 'sports' (if you can call them that) that exploded on the Internet in the early days of social media. What people were discovering was that suddenly, the power of global networking was accelerating what I've come to call the 'big, global idea machine', and that this industry might find opportunities for innovation by tapping into the machine.

In effect, accelerating their diversity of ideas!

I was thinking about this as two articles floated through my news clipping service. One in *Fortune* that outlined how "Walmart Is Launching a Tech Incubator in Silicon Valley," and the second in *Sci-Tech* entitled "Intel's Not the Only Big Company To Find a Self-Driving Partner" which discussed the new partnerships occurring in the world of self-driving car technology.

There are two big issues that are in play here that can be summarized quite nicely:

◆ every industry is becoming a tech industry, and every company is becoming a software company — with the result that companies such as Walmart have to set up in the heart of the tech world in order to get ahead

◆ companies are quickly discovering that they don't have the skills to do what needs to be done, hence, they need to partner up to get things done, which is the key trend occurring in the world of autonomous vehicles right now.

This is echoed by some research I presented in several recent meetings with major private equity investors, based on a study by GE, which found that among senior executives:

◆ 85% are concerned about the velocity introduced by digitization and are open to idea collaboration

◆ 75% indicated they are open to share the revenue stream of an innovation collaboration

◆ 85% indicated such initiatives were growing over the last year.

Key trend? The race for tech skills is going to accelerate; new forms of partnerships will be established faster; lots of money will be made by those who have the requisite skills; and this will be a defining issue for success going forward!

Need a bigger example? This headline: "Ford is putting $1 billion into an AI startup, Detroit's biggest investment yet in self-driving car tech."

Think about that — essentially, it's a billion dollar investment to get the right skills, at the right time, for the right purpose.

Your Strength

*"Your strength will come from the things you do,
not the things you avoid!"*

A ction is far better than inaction — but you know that already.

But when it comes to a difficult challenge, you are probably like many people — you will work hard to avoid doing what is necessary to succeed. You will put off the steps that you should follow to get to a different place. You will not make the decisions that you should be making in order to find some inner peace.

Avoidance must be built into our human DNA, since it seems to be such a common character trait! It is the root cause of so many failures. Give me a list of failures, and I can point to the 'avoidance strategy' at the genesis of the issue.

The Story Behind the Picture

I'm on stage for a company in the medical device industry. Their industry is changing quickly as hyper-connectivity comes to shape the future of their products. They are no longer selling simple devices — they are selling, as I said on stage, some type of 'weird, hyper-connected AI smart thing!"

As with many events, their meeting slogan was: "Stronger." Part of my keynote talked about the need for them to change their approach to selling — in terms of the message, the value proposition, and the way they needed to position this new type of device to their clients. They needed to be stronger in terms of the approach they took to selling this new type of product.

I've seen countless companies fail because they avoid the admission that their competitors have come out with a better solution or product. I've seen them lose market share because senior executives have refused to make the investments necessary to reinvent on a regular basis.

Winners? They don't avoid things — they go at them full speed ahead.

People fail because they have an avoidance virus built into their personal soul. It's easier to follow a path of denial than it is to follow a road of recovery.

But flip it around — take positive actions and things begin to change, often in dramatic fashion. Make decisive change, and stronger changes occur.

You'll also find that your ability to do things you previously imagined were impossible, become possible. The unattainable becomes reachable. The negative becomes a positive.

Continued avoidance provides for an avalanche of failure, while action provides muscle strength for growth.

Taking Initiative

"In the absence of clarity,
taking initiative today is significantly better than
finding a perfect plan tomorrow!"

I had a conversation with a good friend who is struggling with how to align his long term thinking to some pretty significant challenges. Where does he start? How does he stay focused? What should he do?

He's pretty overwhelmed simply by the scale of the long term challenge ahead of him.

That's the same type of conundrum that can hold back many organizations from making progress on some significant opportunities, or aligning themselves to major trends. The future can often seem too overwhelming, fuzzy, unclear.

The Story Behind the Picture

It's from a keynote I did for the 2016 POWDERMET International Conference on Powder Metallurgy and Particulate Materials for the Metal Powder Industries Federation. Yes, that's a mouthful.

But the context of the picture certainly fits the quote and the challenge of aligning long term trends to the necessity for short term action. This group within the manufacturing industry is facing profound change as a result of the most sweeping trends overcoming the sector — 3D printing, aka 'additive manufacturing.' The trend promises to revolutionize the conception and design of products, the materials they are made of and the process used to make them. That's a pretty big change.

While on stage, I spoke about the acceleration of the trends around additive manufacturing, and put into perspective that despite the fact that the disruption that will occur with the trend might be overwhelming, it would be critical to somehow get involved in an aggressive way today. Not necessarily to achieve any great amount of success, but simply, to begin to build up experience and expertise with what this massive trend is all about.

In other words, start small — start now!

That's why rather than thinking long term, it is often best simply to do what is important today. Focus on the small steps, and accomplish the key goals of the moment, rather than letting the complex goals of tomorrow scare you into inaction.

On stage, I'll often close my keynotes with my key phrase, "Think BIG, start small, scale fast!"

The key element in today's quote is that 'start small' component. If you have a good idea of where you need to go, but imprecise information on what you need to do to get there, then simply start taking a whole series of small steps to help to get you going in the right direction! That's something, at least!

When I'm in front of a few thousand people, I can see that the concept in that phrase resonates — people are writing it down, tweeting it, and nodding to each other. Why? It's all too easy to become overwhelmed by the scope of the challenge, which can cause people to freeze with action paralysis. Starting small gives us a way out!

So today? Just do what needs to be done today! Worry about tomorrow, tomorrow!

Same Old Things

"If you keep listening to the same old people,
you'll end up doing the same old things!"

People get stuck in a mono-culture, a sameness of being, a routine of predictability. They end up doing today what they did yesterday, and will do it tomorrow, and will wake up one day and say, "WTF? Why didn't I do anything great with my life?"

Don't do that. It's not a lot of fun.

One of the quickest pathways to failure is getting stuck in a rut. Break out of it. It happens with companies and organizations too. They seek the same old insight, the same old advice, from the same old people, and end up doing the same old things.

The Story Behind the Picture

I was in Phoenix, Arizona for a talk for a group of customers of a global hi-tech company. IT companies are eager to have a regular dialog with key executives in their customer base to talk about their latest product lines, solutions, and services. It is also a good chance for these executives, often the CIO's or CTO's (Chief Information and Chief Technology Officers) of global companies, to network with their peers.

I remember working on this post the morning of my event. The client who brought me in had made a point of booking me instead of the same old type of speakers they usually have for these events — industry representatives, people from research firms spouting the same old statistics about the same old industry trends, sports figures. He was determined that they needed something entirely different (my message) to shake these senior executives out of their lethargy and deal with the fast paced disruptive change impacting their industry today.

I am often contacted by senior executives, "We need to shake things up!" would be their first words, "We really need your insight to get our team to think differently!" Then, they come back with a phrase that is all too common. "We decided to go with an internal speaker." In other words, they are going to hear the same old things, the same old ideas, and would end up doing the same old thing.

One such organization is in the energy industry, which is being energized (pardon the pun) by change. Accelerating changes to the grid, distributed energy concepts, faster renewable science, changing consumer behaviour, the impact of hyperconnectivty. Tomorrow, this company won't look anything like it does today.

It happens all too often. The simple act of seeking my insight would not have changed the world, but it would have indicated the ability to reach beyond themselves to understand what comes next.

Do this today, find someone weird, unique, different, odd. Spend some time with them, and listen to what they have to say. You'll come away with a different perception of the world, and better insight into your future!

Suggestion Boxes

"A suggestion box? That's the best way to trivialize the concept of innovation!"

With 25 years of working with some of the leading organizations in the world on issues related to creativity and innovation, I've seen some of the best and worst approaches to the issue.

The worst approach? An innovation suggestion box! That will doom your efforts from the start!

What are some of the approaches that you can take? What have other successful organizations done?

 Suggestion Boxes

The Story Behind the Picture

This one is from a keynote for the IMX - Interactive Manufacturing Exchange Conference — in Las Vegas. I took a good hard look at the future trends which would impact this sector, challenging the audience that to pick up the pace, they would have to challenge themselves to innovate more in terms of skills, capabilities, methodologies and more.

During the Q&A, one fellow asked me for ideas on how they could heighten the importance of innovation as a concept. I remember responding that one thing he should not do is implement a suggestion box!

Here is a quick list of 10 things that smart, innovative companies do to create an overall sense of innovation-purpose.

◆ Heighten the importance of innovation. One major client with several billions in revenue has eight senior VP's who are responsible for innovation. They don't just walk the talk, they do it. The message to the rest of the company? Innovation is critical — get involved.

◆ Create a compelling sense of urgency. With product lifecycles compressing and markets witnessing fierce competition, now is not the time for studies, committee meetings and reports. It's time for action. Simply do things. Now. Get it done. Analyze it later to figure out how to do it better next time.

◆ Ignite each spark. Innovative leaders know that everyone in the organization has some type of unique creativity and talent. They know how to find it, harness it, and use it to their advantage.

◆ Re-evaluate the mission. You might have been selling widgets five years ago, but the market doesn't want widgets anymore. If the world has moved on, and you haven't, it is time to re-evaluate your purpose, goals and strategies. Rethink the fundamentals in light of changing circumstances.

◆ Build up experiential capital. Innovation comes from risk, and risk comes from experience. The most important asset today isn't found on your balance sheet — it is found in the accumulated wisdom from the many risks that you've taken. The more experiential capital you have, the more you'll succeed.

44

◆ Shift from threat to opportunity. Innovative organizations don't have management and staff who quiver from the fear at what might be coming next. Instead, they're alive from breathing the oxygen of opportunity.

◆ Banish complacency and skepticism. It's all too easy for an organization, bound by a history of inaction, to develop a defeatist culture. Innovative leaders turn this around by motivating everyone to realize that in an era of rapid change, anything is possible.

◆ Innovation osmosis. If you don't have it, get it — that's a good rule of thumb for innovation culture. One client lit a fuse in their innovation culture by buying up small, aggressive, young innovative companies in their industry. They then spent the time to carefully nurture their ideas and harness their creativity.

◆ Stop selling products, and sell results. The word 'solution' is overused and overdone. In a world in which everything is becoming a commodity and everyone is focused on price, change the rules of the game. Refuse to play by thinking about how to play in a completely new game.

◆ Create excitement. I don't know how many surveys I saw this year which indicated that the majority of people in most jobs are bored, unhappy, and ready to bolt. Not at innovative companies! The opportunity for creativity, initiative and purpose results in a different attitude. Where might your organization be on a "corporate happiness index?" If it's low, then you don't have the right environment. Fix that problem — and fix it quick.

It's Possible

"Always live each day believing that the impossible will become possible because it most definitely will!"

Consider that your job is to regularly convince people that the world around them will be completely different in just a few short years and that you'll suggest to them that some of the crazier ideas of science fiction that they are familiar with are about to come true.

They will look at you with disbelief, doubt and in some cases, a derisive laugh. But in the end it will become quite true.

Imagine, for example, the audacious idea that we might one day construct a jet that is lighter than air just like the one that Wonder Woman flies! I presented that idea on stage one day while opening a conference involved with advanced material manufacturing.

The Story Behind the Picture

It's from my keynote for the World Government Summit in Dubai — a massive event with 4,000 attendees from 89 countries and over 120 speakers. I spoke about the accelerating trends which are bringing the future to us faster and the impact that this will have on the opportunity for government organizations to challenge themselves in terms of the big problems and opportunities of our time.

When it comes to education, healthcare, the environment, energy, transit, and many other issues, a wide variety of accelerating trends allow us to think about new solutions to intractable problems!'

My goal on stage was to encourage them to think big and bold about how quickly the world was changing, and the opportunities that it presented.

The audience reaction? I can guarantee you that a number of them thought this was a crazy idea. But it isn't, really, when it comes to the exponentiation of pure science and the rapid emergence of new materials.

We truly live in an extraordinary time when it comes to the rapid evolution of pure science. New materials are developed faster than ever before; collaborative research drives faster discovery; collaborative thinking of a global scale accelerates sharing. There's never been a more exciting time to be a scientist discovering the extraordinary. During my research for this conefrence, I came across some advanced research into the very concept of the Wonder Woman jet. The impossible? Exceedingly possible.

Defeatism

"Deaftism is a drug — you know it's bad for you but you take it because it's the easy way out!"

In the high velocity economy with so much change, people can easily adapt a mindset that 'great things can't happen here!'

Defeatism can be a rampant problem when it comes to business, the economy and obviously, personal issues.

Some people can adopt a mindset that failure is inevitable — that nothing great will ever be accomplished for a wide range of different reasons. The more they think like this, the more they fail. The more they fail, the more they think that they are defeated.

The Story Behind the Picture

After my keynote at the Mississippi Economic Development conference, I led a panel of folks from other jurisdictions who have worked in the field for years. We had a great discussion! One of the issues we talked about was mindset — as in, how can a region like Mississippi battle back against those who think that they might never accomplish something great.

In other words, we focused in on the idea of defeatism.

It becomes an endless cycle. Defeatism as a mindset is a drug. The only way to break free is to take bold steps.

The first step? Recognize the problem and admit that the very idea of defeatism has defeated you and then begin to move on to do something to battle back!

Agility

"Agility is the ability to be adaptable to acceleration!"

Some time back, I did a keynote for the spring meeting of the National Mining Association.

There was a phrase that I had brought into the room: "The future happens slowly, then, all at once!", by Kevin Kelly, the Founder of *Wired*.

It captures the essence of our times — there are any number of trends of significance that we know are going to change the future — but it is difficult to judge when they will become real.

The Story Behind the Picture

The use of the car in the photo is appropriate - it's an electric Tesla. The emergence of electric is going to happen faster than people think and for the mining and other industries that will be raw suppliers, the speed of the change might catch them off guard. Hence, it's a great photo for the context of this quote. Fun thing, this particular photo is from a keynote I had done for a major trucking conference, where I was speaking about the acceleration of trends with self-driving cars!

Think about the speed of change in the automotive industry. Just a few years ago, the predominance of electric vehicle technology was still an idea that was on the margins. Self-driving cars were, by and large, a niche concept talked about only in the far reaches of the industry.

Yet, in as little as a few years, these two concepts will completely change the 100 year old structure, methodology and context of the global automotive industry. And it happened — all at once!

How do trends happen all at once? When it comes to the mining of raw materials, there is unprecedented opportunity with big industry shifts — the acceleration to electric vehicles, battery technology everywhere, the ability to do 3D printing in metal. So too with mining methodology — drones, autonomous trucks, ships and cranes, the Internet of Things (IoT) layered throughout the mine for monitoring and safety. Not to forget digital mapping and location intelligence!

The challenge is to know when to implement any trend, idea, or technology. We know they will be real, we just don't know when. And that's the idea of agility — the ability to suddenly respond and adapt when any particular change 'goes supernova!' In the era of acceleration, anything can happen all at once after being around and 'percolating' for a while.

Offbeat Ideas

"Offbeat ideas are often the best ideas,
because the solution to your problem is
usually not the obvious one!"

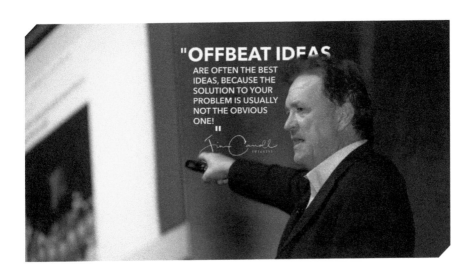

M any times, we'll be boxed in on our thinking on a problem by preconceived notions as to what the question is and we will struggle to find an answer.

This will often lead to investigation paralysis. You'll become bogged down if you can't find a quick answer to your question.

My solution? Ask a different question! Change the question. Start with a different question.

The Story Behind the Picture

I had a friend go for a summer holiday with her family in Newfoundland, Canada. For some reason which mystifies me, they forgot to arrange for a car rental. Given that it's the busiest tourist season on "The Rock," availability was scarce. She put out a plea for transportation ideas on Facebook. While many people suggested she contact other people to see if they might have any ideas, I told her to contact U-Haul. They've got vehicles, they're cheap, and they are probably available. They were. Problem solved!

The thing is, she thought she was looking for a *car* rental company but she was really looking for a *transportation* rental company. She just needed to change the question.

Just be different in your approach to the question — and the logical conclusion of such a thought process is that the answer to your question will be entirely different, once you start with an entirely different question!

It also goes to the idea of asking better questions!

Ask yourself different questions, and seek the non-obvious answers. The results might astound you!

Create The Future

"Worrying about your future won't prevent it.
Doing something about it will let you create it!"

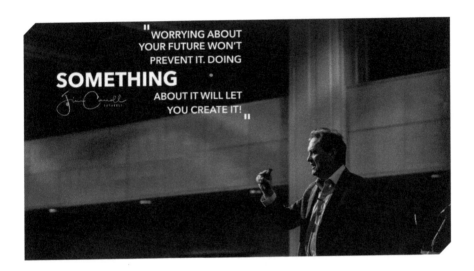

Imagine that you have a job in which you get to freak people out on a regular basis!

No, not @AliceCooper — me!

You should witness some of the audience reactions I see at times when I'm up on the stage. Worry, concern, fear, shock, stress — I can see it in the faces of some of those in the crowd. But that's the minority, the rest seem to display enthusiasm, smiles, an understanding that they are on the right track.

The Story Behind the Picture

The food industry parallels many others. The faster arrival of new taste trends. Ever more fickle consumers. Fleeting attention spans. Marketing and branding messages which need to be continually updated, or they look old and tired.

Part of my message to the audience at this food conference had to do with the fast emerging trend involving food, science, genomic medicine and mobile devices — and a new emerging opportunity that involves 'highly customizable, programmable food consumption.' The whole idea being that increasingly, you will eat 'who you are' based on your particular genetic profile

I could see a couple of folks a few rows in, with a discernible look of fear and concern on their faces. I drew into that, and began to spin my remarks on the trend to speak directly to them, acknowledging their worry, speaking to their concern, and indicating that it isn't unusual to react in such a way. But emphasizing that change is inevitable!

Why the different responses? Simply put, some people do not like the future. They don't like what it represents, fear the change it brings, are apprehensive of the disruption it will cause, and are worried about how they will cope. They're not in the right mindset and didn't really hear what I said in the opening minutes of my talk: "Some people see the future and see a threat. Innovators see the same trend and see an opportunity!"

Those who are in the right mindset are busy taking apart the trend and figuring out how to work with it, shape it, embrace it.

The fearful ones? They are busy trying to determine how to build a barrier around the trend, avoid it, ignore it, complain about it. What a depressing bunch!

But I never give up, as I continue to work to bring the fearful ones over to the other side of hope, enthusiasm, insight and opportunity.

Achieve Success!

"The best way to achieve success in the future is to actually make the effort to go there!"

What I've learned from 25 years on the stage is that some people will blame everyone else but themselves for their lack of success. And when failure comes, it is the fault of everyone else! The quote captures the essence of their mindset.

Take the issue of 'trade barriers' which has come about as the result of an increasingly chaotic political environment over the last several years. It seems that some believe that with a wave of a magic wand, an entire industry can be transformed overnight and returned to its former glory.

The Story Behind the Picture

The photo is from a pretty ironic place to be delivering a keynote on the topic of the future of manufacturing — at the Trump Doral Resort in Miami — at the same time that trade barriers were being put in place to try to take an industry back to where it was in the 1950's.

It's pretty easy to think about the context of the inspiration for the quote!

But the future doesn't happen like that — there are no magic solutions for success.

How does the future come about? Through constant innovation, big bold moves, skill set reinvention and challenging thinking that will, and already is, providing for significant transformation.

Take the world of manufacturing, it's all about: adapting to collapsing product lifecycles and reinventing products faster; redefining products through the connectivity and intelligence that comes through the Internet of Things (IoT) connectivity; process change such as mass customization; digitization, robotics and the cloud. Then there are opportunities for design that come from crowd thinking and crowd-sourcing, as well as through rapid prototyping and faster deployment. Not to forget massive new opportunities from 3D printing or additive manufacturing.

All of those changes present opportunities but also involve a tremendous amount of hard work. Does that work for everyone? Not at all — there are always those who are in the frame of mind that by trying to stop the future you can return to the past.

In other words they are likely doomed to fail in the future because they will make little effort to actually get there!

Your Vision!

"Don't bore me with your excuses on why it can't be done. Excite me with your vision of how it will be done!"

I t's best to counter negativity with action — that's long been my guiding principle!

The fact is, it's easier to be negative than it is to be positive and not just at a personal level.

Negativity inherently leads to excuses, because that is the easy way out!

The Story Behind The Picture

The particular phrase came to mind one day as I spent some time talking with a good friend who was struggling with some unique challenges in his career path. Any time that there is a difficult change in circumstances, it is extremely easy to let negativity creep in and to let disparaging thoughts be the guiding factor.

I remember what I went through when I did a career change and jumped out on my own almost 30 years ago. It was terrifying, inspiring, motivating and overwhelming all at the same time. But looking back, it was the smartest thing I ever did. Today, I have clients all around the world looking to me for my unique skills, guidance, and insight. Heck, even NASA had me in to access my brain— twice!

But I had to constantly battle against the negativity. I remember at the time that I was really effective at coming up with a list of my shortcomings and not enough of a list of my strengths. Looking back, I now know that I should have been more focused on the latter!

It's a line of thinking that clients who I deal with face almost everyday. I deal with Fortune 500 global organizations, where senior executives are full of excuses on why they might not be able to deal with the massive business model disruption occurring in their industry. I often don't see enough in terms of flashes of brilliance or big, bold thinking on how they will turn the tables around and be the disruptor.

As for you — what are you going to do today to turn your inventory of excuses into a treasure chest of enthusiasm?

Disrupt Amazon!

"Disrupt Amazon! Turn your strategy upside down, and turn the predictable response into the unexpected!"

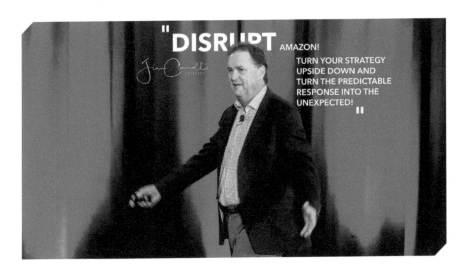

In more industries than you think, Amazon is the elephant in the room. My experience has taught me that in every single industry, regardless of what you do and what you sell, you are or will soon be faced with a situation in which Amazon will challenge your business model, and shake your belief in the future to the core.

What do you do as this situation comes about?

Don't wait for Amazon to disrupt you — disrupt yourself and disrupt Amazon first!

The Story Behind the Picture

This particular photo is from an event with several hundred insurance brokers. Might Amazon disrupt the world of insurance? It's certainly possible. The phrase used for this type of disruption carries the fancy term "disintermediation." It simply means that the middleman is cut out of a business relationship.

The fact is, Amazon (and other companies with the same strategy as Amazon) isn't just changing the world of retail, it's changing and challenging virtually every type of business that involves a middleman.

With that, in the last few years I've been called into an increasing number of events where this is the new reality going forward — with clients seeking insight on what they should do when their business model is under threat. In quite a few of these events, I'm asked to address the 'elephant in the room', which is Amazon.

My key message? Don't compete — transform!

When Amazonian scale disruption occurs, you can't hope to compete on price, the sophistication of the online interaction, or the other areas in which Amazon (and similar disruptors) clearly excel. You need a different proposition, different ideas and a different strategy.

In many cases, this will come about through an implicit decision to compete based on the unique value you can bring to the relationship — service, support, personal interaction and other factors. In doing so, you specifically choose to not compete based on price.

The examples of the challenge are manyfold. I was invited in to speak at the quarterly leadership meeting of a company that is one of the leaders in the medical supplies marketplace. Clearly, a good chunk of their business could be subjected to risk as Amazon gets into their line of business.

How do they survive? Not by trying to offer a better price, but by working to ensure that their sales and professional representatives are working harder to provide greater value on the service relationship they have with their clients.

Another example are agricultural dealers who sell products to farmers. The simplistic view is that they buy products from the manufacturer and then sell them to the farmer, with an obvious markup in price. Amazon could do this (and will) with a more sophisticated online system and avoid the cost of the markup, thereby offering a lower cost alternative. How to compete? Become an invaluable partner to the farmer in terms of advice, expertise and personal support for new initiatives, products and ideas. Don't hope to compete on price — because you will watch your business disappear!

The "Amazonification of industries" can get even more complex than that when Amazon decides to offer a service element too! This is coming about quickly in the home repair industry. Buy a door or window on Amazon and they'll line you up with a contractor that will do the installation for you. How can you compete if you are an established home contractor with a successful operation? It's not an easy question, but is a reality that you might need to address!

Optimists!

"Surround yourself with optimists.
Always ignore the pessimists!"

Some of the most fascinating organizations in the world have brought me in to encourage their people to think about the future and how to nurture a culture of creativity and innovation. Organizations like NASA (twice!), Johnson and Johnson, Whirlpool/Maytag, the Walt Disney Corporation and literally hundreds more!

One of my key motivational points for my clients has always been this idea: "Many people see a trend and see a threat. Smart people see the same trend and see opportunity"

The Story Behind the Picture

*I'm on stage in Orlando, speaking at a conference of association executives —
individuals who manage large sized professional, industry or trade associations.*

*They are faced with a tremendous amount of challenge and change: a declining
membership base, lower attendance at their annual conference or trade show, and
a generation of millennials who don't always find it necessary to join an association
because they network in different ways.*

*These trends mean that within the professional association industry, there is
currently a LOT of negative thinking, and some people who are convinced that the
glory days of the association industry are over. Not if it is reinvented and transformed
— and so that was a part of my message and the genesis for the quote.*

Think about that and then ask yourself how you keep yourself in an innovative
frame of mind.

A good part of it has to do with the company you keep! To that end, I'd suggest
that you surround yourself with:

◆ Optimists. You need to hang out with people who see all kinds of
opportunity — not gloomsters who are convinced there is no future
out there!

◆ People who do. Action oriented people. Folks who accomplish things.
Those that do.

◆ People with open minds. Innovators aren't prepared to accept the status
quo — they are willing to explore and understand different viewpoints,
and use that as a kickoff for creativity.

◆ People who have experienced failure. Innovation comes from risk; risk
comes from trying things. Try lots of things and many will fail. That's
good. That builds up experience, which gives you better insight into a
fast paced world.

◆ Oddballs and rebels. Some of the most brilliant thinking and best ideas
can come from those who view the world through a different lens. They
may seem odd at times, but they can be brilliantly creative.

◆ Good listeners and debaters. They're willing to challenge ideas, analyze
issues and think through the possibilities.

◆ People who think differently than you do. If you really want to be innovative, go to two conferences a year that have nothing to do with what you do. You'll be amazed at what you learn and how it will re-stir your creative juices.

In every single keynote, I focus on future trends and opportunities and link that to the process and mindset of innovation. I'm an optimist, continually trying new things, listening to other people, watching, observing, and listening.

Most important, I refuse to give in to the pervasive negative thinking that so many people seem to envelope themselves within. Maybe that's why I see so many opportunities in today's economy.

Think growth!

Arrogance Kills!

"Arrogance kills!"

One of the sins that will guarantee your failure is complacency: a belief that your world won't change.

At the other extreme, arrogance — a belief that while your world will change, you are so strong and impervious that you won't be impacted.

Complacency in the face of massive business model disruption is a pretty bad state to be in, but arrogance is much worse. Sadly, I see it within many of the clients that I deal with, often at the most senior levels of the organization.

The Story Behind the Picture

I've come to tell the story on stage of one client that is, in essence, a middleman wholesaler — they simply sell products from manufacturers to end customers. They are ripe for massive disruption by Amazon, and it's pretty likely their business model will be ripped apart and reassembled in as little as 10 years.

My keynote focused on the need to enhance their client relationships so that they weren't just selling a widget anymore; that they needed to bring more value to the relationship, because in the world of Amazon, you are just competing on price.

After I left the stage, the CEO got up and basically discounted everything I had just said. "We'll be fine," was his message. "We own our markets, and we always will."

I remember looking at the senior VP who had arranged to have me come in. He had a look of horror on his face! He knew, and I knew, that the company really had to change what it sold, and how it sold it, to survive in a future of Amazonian disruption!

Today, I'm seeing more news reports that are suggesting the future I prophesied on stage is coming true with pretty staggering speed. I predict that in just a few years, the CEO will be gone, the destructive impact of his arrogance having run its course.

I've seen this over and over and over again. I was with Motorola in 2006, for a global R&D meeting where I suggested that maybe Apple and others might enter the cellular phone business in which Motorola currently had an edge.

They said the Razr model, then the best selling phone in the world, would always be supreme.

Oops!

Arrogance. It will always get you in the end!

Define Your Goals!

*"Define the scope of your goals
by the size of your dreams!"*

It's really easy to think small!

That's because being small involves the easiest of all decisions — it doesn't require one!

Small goals involve only a little bit of change, don't carry a lot of effort, and as a result are easy to accomplish. On the other hand, you won't get much done, and certainly won't get an overall sense of accomplishment.

The Story Behind the Picture

It's from a manufacturing conference in Chicago, but it could be any one of my many keynotes over the last many years. It's my closing slide and the inspiration for the title of this book!

I've found it useful to leave my audience with one great, wrap-up closing thought and found the formula one day when I pulled together the "Think Big, Start Small, Scale Fast" structure. At that point, from the stage, I could see people writing down the phrase as a great takeaway, an inspirational thought for them to begin to work the concepts and trends that I had outlined in my talk.

Big goals, on the other hand, involve hard work. Big projects take commitment, courage, determination, risk, intense focus, the right mindset. All the things that make them big in scope and challenging to think about!

Yet, you'll get more from pursuing a big idea or massive goal, because even if you only get part of the way there, you end up with a better return on your motivational investment.

Many people and companies though, are structured for small. They are bound up in tradition, process, certain defined ways of doing things — rules — that have helped them succeed in the past.

Over time, they have developed a corporate culture which might have worked at the smaller idea world of the past, but now has them on the sick-bed, suffering from an organizational sclerosis that clogs up their ability to try to do anything new.

Those very things which worked for them in the past are the anchors that now hold them back as the future rushes at them, being redefined by those who are prepared to think big!

What's the way out? By thinking big and bold! Taking your dreams and trying to turn them into reality. Refusing to limit yourself by being small!

Enthusiasm Is Everything!

"Your enthusiasm is everything!"

This idea actually came from one of my sisters one morning shortly after she saw one of these daily motivational quotes that I post.
She sent me one from author Roald Dahl:

> *"I began to realize how important it was to be an enthusiast in life…. if you are interested in something, no matter what it is, go at it at full speed ahead. Embrace it with both arms, hug it, love it and above all become passionate about it.*
> *Lukewarm is no good."*

The Story Behind the Picture

I was invited to keynote the Oklahoma City Chamber of Commerce. It's a region that is buffeted by profound change, particularly as the oil and energy economy undergoes a significant transition as renewables take hold.

It's easy for people in such an economic region to lose sight of opportunity, and from that, their focus on the future.

And so I found myself suddenly using this idea on stage, "Your enthusiasm for the future will define your future!"

At the end of my talks, I'll often talk to the audience about the need to fully embrace the future rather than shying away from it; turn trends into opportunities instead of viewing them as threats; and using creativity as a tool rather than utilizing inaction as a crutch.

Her comment was that my enthusiasm for everything as found in my quotes about the future seemed somewhat infectious! I get similar feedback from others on a regular basis. People like to be inspired by enthusiasm!

Given the speed of change in our world today — in industries, careers, organizations, and in our personal lives — enthusiasm is often the energy that can get us through.

If you are going to have to deal with some challenge and change, there is no good that will come from going at it half-speed. You've got to give it all you've got and never lose sight of the goal.

Shared Ideas!

"The best ideas are shared ideas!"

Many of the global leadership events that I am brought into have a specific focus on how to use the power of internal collaboration within an organization to achieve innovation; how to better develop an internal collaborative culture within the organization; or to discuss the opportunities that history has taught us that come from successful collaboration.

The issue of collaboration has long been a key goal of corporate culture initiatives and yet seems to be elusive in terms of success. Organizations have built in structural barriers which kill collaborative thinking; private power fiefdoms often doom such efforts; people are often rewarded based on individual results rather than team efforts.

The Story Behind the Picture

The photo was taken during my keynote for Pladis (formerly Godiva/McVitie's/ Ulker) in London, UK.

The fact that Einstein is in there is great; I often use his observation that "insanity is doing the same thing over and over again, and expecting a different result each time." That's a great quote about innovation!

But that's not the focus of my quote. The quote is all about the fact that organizations that manage to create a culture in which ideas float freely throughout the organization generally achieve greater success with innovation.

Yet in the face of such barriers, proof exists that organizations which excel at internal information sharing are those who win in the long run.The power of collaborative thinking comes from the unique energy that forms from synergistic ideas.

There is no doubt that collaboration is critical. In fact I wrote about the issues that are cruical to overall innovation success in a blogpost a few years ago. The post was entitiled the "Six C's of Innovation", the others being curiosity, creativity, change oriented, courage and the ability to create excitement every day!

Focus on creating a culture of collaboration — you'll find it to be one of the most powerful things that you can do!

Perfection

"Perfection is the enemy of innovation."

In my list of global clients, I encounter far too many people and leaders who subscribe to the idea that if they are going to do something, they need to do it absolutely perfectly the first time around.

In my view, this doesn't fit within the fast economy of today. Take a look around at successful innovators, they are willing to do something fast, see how it worked, and try again. Obviously quality and risk issues come into play but they manage that by innovating within their quality validation process.

The Story Behind the Picture

This one is from an agricultural conference in New Orleans.

I have a room full of farmers and just pointed out that there is a lot of crowdfunding research going on within their industry, particularly with agricultural robotics and self-driving vehicles. I point out that the very nature of crowdfunding research relies on fast innovation, iterative design, and seeking goals that aren't an end goal but mere intermediate steps on the journey to a conclusion.

The whole idea of 'getting things right the first time' is going out the window with new trends.

The best way is to understand how manufacturing is changing with 3D printing. We now have the ability to conceive a product, design it, build it, test it, and then re-conceive, re-design and re-deploy it. Product design has become an iterative process instead of a final step process.

The entire concept of abandoning first-step perfect is accelerated by the instant feedback of the internet and the concept of the never-ending 'beta' so perfectly mastered by the likes of Google. Companies can put out an early prototype of a product or a service and seek a small (or large) group of testers willing to explore, kick the tires, and provide feedback.

Here's the thing: the future is happening faster. Trends are accelerating. You need to get there quicker. One of the ways to do so is to challenge yourself when it comes to quality.

Ambition!

"If complacency is the killer, ambition is the antidote!"

IF COMPLACENCY IS THE KILLER,
AMBITION
IS THE ANTIDOTE!

see complacency all the time in my 'day job.' There are lots of organizations who think that their business model will be the same in ten years, that they'll face the same competitors and will sell the same type of product.

They won't.

I've seen CEO's of global, multi-billion dollar companies explain that they are somehow 'different,' and won't be buffeted by the ill winds of change. I've talked to people who have explained to me that their strategy from yesterday will work perfectly fine in a different world tomorrow. I've met individuals who are convinced that some of the 'crazy ideas' floating around in their industry won't go anywhere and that they can easily relax.

The Story Behind the Picture

The photo is from a keynote I gave in the utility and energy sector — a room full of executives responsible for your local electrical utility.

This industry is undergoing a tremendous amount of change and it's fair to say that it will see more change in the next five years than in the previous century. Renewable energy sources, battery power, the Internet of Things (IoT), electric vehicles, skills shortages, new ways of working and changing business models are just a few of the changes that are transforming the industry. All this is happening in the context of an industry that is historically slow to move and react — after all, the electrical grid has not changed for a long time.

It is this type of industry in which complacency can certainly settle in, which is why my message focuses on what energy providers can do to thrive, not just survive, amid constant market disruption and change.

Right.

The problem with this type of attitude is that it brings about the evil drug known as complacency, with the dangerous side effects of inaction, loss of focus, organizational sclerosis, cumbersome actions and lumbering, ponderous strategies. All not really in the best long term health for the organization!

The business world doesn't take kindly to that type of behaviour anymore.

Neither does your personal life! When things are easy, it's easy to be caught off guard. It's only when it becomes complex that your survival instincts kick in, often in a rush of panic.

Why not avoid the panic stage and do the things you need to do when you should be doing them?

Acceleration

"Expect velocity. Plan for acceleration.
Structure for intensity. Execute relentlessly."

Are you thinking fast enough? Are you structured for speed? Are you wired for velocity?

You'll catch my drift that I think one of the most critical things we can do in organizations today is to prepare and align ourselves to the faster future. The quote above captures the essence of that thinking.

The Story Behind the Picture

The picture is actually from a keynote that I did for a global conference held in Sao Paolo, Brazil! But the thought process involving the use of the photo for my quote came about because someone was on my Web site that particular morning. They were reading an article that I had written after I had keynoted the Society of Cable Telecom Engineers at their annual conference in Tampa in 2006. The title of the article? "Are You Thinking Fast Enough?" (It's still on my Web site).

At the time, YouTube was only just beginning to have an impact, and social networking was still in a nascent stage. It was January 2006 — Twitter wasn't even around!

As opening keynote, I was to get them in the right, innovative frame of mind to deal with an upcoming tsunami of change. My job was to alert them that forthcoming trends would mean that they would be faced with the need to accelerate the bandwidth on their networks. I spoke to the trends I predicted in my book of 1999, Light Bulbs to Yottabits, which took a look at the forthcoming world of online video.

The article still makes for good reading today, starting with the observation that "in this era in which new developments and technology are coming to the market faster than ever before, everyone must become an innovator, whether it be with new business models, skills partnerships or customer solutions."

With that thought in mind, it's worthwhile revisiting what I had suggested in an article I wrote in 2006, *Are You Thinking Fast Enough?* and consider what has transpired since:

- ◆ **Hyper-innovation dominates.** New business models, new products, new ideas. Old thinking went out the window as young upstarts redefined the world.

- ◆ **Furious rates of scientific advance would dominate our world.** Consider what has happened in the world of energy, as renewables have began to overtake carbon sources of energy generation, to such a degree that most people now recognize that 'oil is over'.

- ◆ **Product lifecycles disappear.** We would soon see the emergence of the iPhone and the appearance of more than 10 different models of the device over a 10 year time span.

- ◆ **New competitors will continue to emerge at a furious pace overnight.** After the article? Uber, AirBnB and other major companies, and the world 'business model disruption' came to dominate our thinking.

- **Products continue to commoditize and service, integration and delivery are key.** Amazon became a competitor to everyone and companies tried to survive by focusing on service rather than price.

- **Skills agility is key.** Companies began to scramble for skills. Car companies suddenly had to become experts in battery technology as a rush to EV's began to occur. They also realized they didn't have the right people with the necessary skills in place.

- **Generational mindset drive faster change.** Folks like Elon Musk came to reinvent entire industries, driven by their embrace of technology driven change.

- **Customer expectations accelerate.** Overnight, review sites like Yelp began to dominate the selection of products and services and bad service became a death sentence.

Those are still the defining trends for many organizations today.

Agility, innovation and execution are critical. They are three little words that carry an immense amount of guidance and insight for savvy executives to base their strategies on as they carry themselves into the future.

Need For Speed!

"Those who succeed possess a daring need for speed!"

One of my key themes through the years has been that "faster is the new fast" — that the biggest challenge that organizations must face is how to keep up with the high-velocity economy.

I'm now observing that in many markets and industries, the pace of change is so fast that we need to put in place a senior executive whose sole area of responsibility is ensuring that the organization can keep up with ever-increasing rate of change.

Let's say — a Chief Momentum Officer (CMO)!

The Story Behind the Picture

I'm on stage in Chicago speaking at a manufacturing conference and it's the opening moments of my talk.

For years, I've been using a quote at the start of my talk that relates to the theme that "the future belongs to those who are fast." The traffic blur picture on the screen behind me is part of my keynote where I emphasize this issue.

In my hand I'm holding an iPhone and talking about how quickly we replace these devices, as well as how fast they evolve and change. I then tell the story that the relatively fast product lifecycle of the smartphone is coming to every industry!

Organizations need to adapt to all kinds of different issues when it comes to the velocity of change — rapidly changing business models, the emergence of new competitors, ever shrinking product lifecycles, a faster pace of new product development, furious rates of technological innovation, furiously fast new trends in terms of customer interaction, the decreasing shelf-life of knowledge and the more rapid emergence of specialized skills, the list could go on! Hence, there is a need for someone who can align all of the moving parts of the organization to high velocity change!

This individual will carry a number of responsibilities, such as:

◆ managing the product innovation pipeline, so that the organization has a constant supply of new, innovative products, as existing products become obsolete, marginalized, or unprofitable

◆ managing the talent pipeline, so that the organization has the ability to quickly ingest all kinds of specialized new skills

◆ managing the technology pipeline, so that the organization can adapt itself to constantly improving and ever-more sophisticated IT tools that will help to better manage, run, grow and transform the business

◆ maintain and continually enhance brand and corporate image; brands can become "tired" and irrelevant if they aren't continually refreshed

◆ ensuring that the organization is continuing to explore new areas for opportunity and that it has the right degrees of innovation momentum

◆ that the business processes and structure of the organization are fine-tuned on a continuous basis so that it can keep up with all the fast-change swirling around it

◆ ensuring that a sufficient number of "experiential" programs are underway with respect to product, branding, markets, and other areas so that the overall expertise level of the organization is continually enhanced.

In other words, the CMO has two key responsibilities:

◆ keeping a fine tuned eye on the trends which will impact the organization in the future and which will serve to increase the velocity that the organization is subjected to and;

◆ keeping their hands on the appropriate levers throughout the organization such that it can keep evolving at the pace that these future trends will demand.

I don't know if that makes perfect sense, but I think it's a good issue to think about.

Personal Moonshot

"We live in an era in which someone has launched their own car to Mars.
What's your personal moonshot?"

You can't help but be captivated by the audacity and daring of Elon Musk, and his initiatives with SpaceX, Tesla and the GigaFactory. He is busy reinventing entire industries!

Not to mention the drama that comes from launching a car into space! In doing so, he follows a bold concept known as 'moonshot thinking' — define your boldest goal and pursue it. Emulate the big-thinking of the 1960's as found with NASA and the moon landings.

The Story Behind the Picture

I was on a plane on my way to Dubai. Just before my departure, SpaceX had launched its Falcoln 9 Heavy rocket and Elon Musk had the audacity to place his Tesla Roadster in the nose cone. The photograph which was beamed down from the heavens and caught the attention of the world, was that of the Starman sitting in the Tesla on the way to Mars.

It was only natural that my quote of the day would use that concept.

With moonshot thinking, no goal is too big — everything is potentially within reach.

Moonshot thinking is transforming entire industries. There are moonshots involving some of the biggest problems, challenges and opportunities of our time, having to do with education, healthcare, the environment, and obviously, conquering and colonizing space! Certainly the ones getting the most attention are those involving the space industry, with tech titans getting most of the attention: Jeff Bezos from Amazon Blue Origin space initiative, and Richard Branson's VirginGalactic project, in addition to Elon Musk.

Yet there are many others, such as moonshots for a cure for cancer as announced by Vice President Joe Biden a few years ago.

Moonshots are big and bold, it is said that it is finding success somewhere between science fiction and emerging technology. It doesn't involve small incremental steps, but massive transformative goals. The concept of the self-driving car? It originally came from a DARPA (Defense Advanced Research Projects Agency) challenge to develop a vehicle that could go from coast-to-coast in the US on its own — a challenge that led to the fast development of a lot of technology and a lot of thinking on what this challenge might lead to.

When it comes to your own mindset, maybe you should adopt your own personal moonshot. Find and adopt the greatest challenge in your lifetime and pursue it with passion!

Tradition

"Maybe your worst enemy is tradition!"

People love to cling to routine. They glue themselves to the past. They are relentless in their focus on their success from yesterday. They chain themselves to their legacy rather than working to define themselves a new one.

And in doing so, they forget that tomorrow will be, as it is said, a different day. When it arrives with full, disruptive, unrelenting force, they are fully unprepared! "Whoah, where did that come from?" they echo.

Traditions are the enemy of innovation and creativity, because they bind us to routine. They plant us in the warmth of comfort rather than the chill of discomfort — the latter can wake you up and force you to get moving!

The Story Behind the Picture

National Cowboy Museum in Oklahoma City. What a great spot to think about both the promise and perils of tradition and reliance on the glories of the past!

I've come to believe that much of the political discourse in our world today is coming from people who believe that the past was so great that we should preserve that way of life and manner of thinking as a pathway into the future.

Traditions can be innovation and creative poison, because it can cause organizations and people to be too caught up in the past, which causes them to lose sight of opportunities for the future.

Tradition can get people to think too much about the ideas that created the glories of the past, rather than the new ideas which are necessary for tomorrow.

The future doesn't really agree with that frame of mind! It has its own disruptive, transformative concepts as to how things will be entirely different.

Don't get me wrong, I'm a big fan of tradition when it is used at the right purpose, at the right time, for the right form of inspiration.

I just believe that overt reliance upon tradition is a dangerous thing. And so when it comes to your own traditions, you should define a new one, or transform and change existing ones.

Scared Of The Future

"People aren't scared of the future!
They're terrified of new and unfamiliar ideas!"

The concept of the 'comfort zone' is kind of a dumb idea. After all, how can you ever be comfortable if the world around you is constantly shifting, changing, becoming unrecognizable moment by moment?

You recoil in fear and try to retreat into the cocoon of your comfort zone. Yet, that won't last too long, because the change will eventually capture and smother you with the unfamiliar.

That's a bit of a problem if you don't have the right mindset!

The Story Behind the Picture

I'm on stage at Microsoft's FutureNow event, a massive conference focused on new technologies, disruptive change and forward oriented thinking. There are a lot of information technology people in the room, from CIO's (Chief Information Officers) to folks who are 'down in the trenches,' responsible for the implementation of a lot of technology in major organizations.

These people are at the forefront of change as they are the ones driving it. Much of what they do — putting in place sophisticated IT technology — is a necessary evil, as organizations come to put in place the infrastructure that drives their future. And yet, their very actions cause concern, worry and fear and so part of my message to them was that they need to work a little bit harder to ease the concern of those who are impacted.

What if you could make your fear go away through better insight? If you know what is coming next, wouldn't you have a better opportunity to align yourself to it?

On stage, I'll often speak about the need for an effective form of 'personal future insight,' or what I call your 'personal trends radar.' You develop one to enhance your ability to see the obvious and plan for it accordingly. Much of what will happen in the future is already around us and so many aspects of the future are blindingly obvious.

How do you develop this radar? Much of it has to do with the company that you keep on a day to day basis.

Do you live inside a 'fear bubble' that is constantly reinforced by those around you? Change it. Hang out with optimists, innovators, positive minded people, individuals who are busy designing the future and those who are focused on the opportunity of what comes next.

Avoid the negative people — the downers, the whiners, the complainers, skeptics, and anti-science losers. These folks have a future anti-virus engineered into their DNA. Spend time with them and you'll be guaranteed to live a life of fear with what comes next, while what comes next is going to happen to you anyways!

If you spend more time understanding what comes next and prepare yourself for it, the issue of fear from unfamiliar ideas pretty much disappears!

Bigger Problems

*"If everyone around you is saying
'we don't need to do that right now,'
you have bigger problems than you think!"*

You are probably already nodding your head in agreement because you are surrounded by people who are driven by a compelling lack of urgency.

I see it all the time in my line of work and I actually feel bad for many of the potential clients that approach me to come in for a talk. A senior executive will find me, often online or by word of mouth, and call me with great excitement to explore how I can help them move forward with their initiatives. We have a great discussion around the ways that I will kick their innovation efforts into high gear and accelerate their capabilities.

The Story Behind the Picture

I'm on stage at a healthcare conference. The challenges in heathcare are vast — massive spending based on demographic change and increasing demand, fewer resources, skills challenges and more. If there is any industry that should have a sense of urgency to deal with the scope of challenges that exists, it's this one!

In this case, I'm speaking about the fact that some companies and people are looking at big, bold ideas — such as the concept of a medical tricorder from StarTrek — as potential opportunities to deal with the scope of the challenges that exist. The idea is to use technology to provide for 'virtualized care.'

Certainly this idea of extending the reach of a hospital or medical institution into a community through remote patient monitoring technology provides a huge opportunity for innovation. And yet I know from this particular event, that there seemed to be a huge lack of urgency in the room, staggering compancency, and massive inertia. Think about it — massive problems, big opportunities and it seems that the two might never meet!

Because, excited with the potential to get things moving, they take it to their 'team' or their boss, and the answer comes back: "We don't need to do it right now." Initiative is left dead, dying on the tracks, smothered by complacency.

This happens far more often than you might believe. So much so, that I wrote a blog post around the trend: "What does it mean when your CEO says we don't need to do that right now?"

It means that your organization is dying from a compelling lack of urgency.

If you don't prepare for the future now, when do you? After it happens? That doesn't make a lot of sense. And yet, countless people and organizations do exactly that. Then, they sit back and complain with astonishment: "Whoah, I didn't see that coming."

But you should have, because the future is happening all around us, right now, at this very moment

Dream Big!!

"Don't be afraid of dreaming too big.
Be afraid of thinking too small!"

When everything around you is transforming at a furious pace, one of the worst things that you can do is to limit your thinking!

After all, history is full of heroes who have thought really big about their future, the potential scope of the new industries and business operations that they might push into, and the business models they might put in place. Richard Branson redefined the music, airline and rail industries. Elon Musk reinvented concepts in the automative industry, the energy and battery industry through the GigaFactory and took on the business of launching rockets with his SpaceX venture.

The Story Behind the Picture

I've spoken at numerous events in the agriculture sector, groups of famers and producers, global agricultural companies and local cooperatives, as well as various professional and industry associations.

All of this has involved a regular effort to keep up with the trends impacting the world of agriculture. My involvement with the industry over a 25 year time span has demonstrated that everyone in the industry has been inundated with a constant influx of ideas, faster science, new methodologies and all kinds of new technologies and concepts.

All of this is happening in the context of a need to continue increasing the overall yield on the average farm to keep up with global demand — it is estimated that global food production has to double to keep up, while little new arable land is coming to market. This means that existing food producers need to continually improve their yield and production.

During the keynote, I related the story that there are really two different types of farmers in the agricultural industry and made the point to the audience that their attitude towards innovation should be considered in the light of the attitudes carried by each type of farmer.

The first type of farmer is what we might call the 'apathetic minority,' who share these attributes:

- *they are not optimistic about the future*
- *they tend to seek the "same old advice" from the "same old sources"*
- *they have a high intolerance for risk*
- *they're not convinced they can continue to make a comfortable living despite all the contrary evidence*
- *they're skeptical of their potential since they feel they've seen too many ups and downs in the industry*

Then there is the second group we might call the 'future positive' type of farmer. They share these attributes :

- *they're quite optimistic about the future*
- *they're very business minded, using all the latest tools and ideas at their disposal*
- *they are very innovation oriented, willing to approach everything in a new way with new ideas*
- *they are very collaborative for advice, seeking ideas from anyone and everyone*

• they're often focused on planning, profit, growth, with
clear objectives in mind
What's common to this second type of farmer is that they are fully prepared to think big and bold in terms of the future of agriculture, particularly with respect to the need to double production. The result is that they don't hold themselves back in terms of thinking big and dreaming big!

So here's a good question: when it comes to you, or the organization that you work for, what type of farmer are you? Are your dreams big enough?

While we all can't be a Branson or a Musk, we can make a conscious decision to not limit our thinking and our dreams, otherwise complacency and inertia can settle in and you won't be stirred on to do the things that you need to do to keep up with a faster world.

Don't let the idea of thinking 'big' hold you back. Thinking big is a critical element to any type of success and need not be earth shattering in scope! Often times, it can be just enough to push you on to pursue a potentially crazy idea. Indeed, just as I was writing this section, I had a LinkedIn invitation from none other than Devon Carter — one of the original members of the Jamaican Bobsled team.

Now that's thinking big!

Progress Is Great!

"The attitude of some people is that while progress is great, it has gone on way too long. The future won't pay any attention to that type of thinking!"

A quote I often use on stage, which neatly summarizes the dilemma that people face when it comes to a faster future, dramatic, disruptive trends and what seems like an unforgiving rate of change.

The Story Behind the Picture

I know that many people in my audiences are uncomfortable with the future and change, so there is always a careful balance between putting into perspective the reality of the trends which come next and motivating them to a mindset that will help them to align to those trends.

It usually works — I get rave reviews! You can't survive in this industry for this long if you don't.

But only once in 25 years have I encountered an overtly hostile audience. It was an internal leadership meeting for a major government agency in the agricultural field, specifically a number of mid-level managers from the Midwest of the US. My talk focused on the reality of the future of agriculture: trends such as accelerated science, the impact of genomics, precision farming ... Fitbits for cows!

They would have none of it! I could see fear, terror and even anger in the room from the stage. I was presenting the reality of a faster future to people who clearly wanted to have nothing to do with it. I realized right then that in the room I had a group of folks who would obviously prefer that the world stay where it was, and indeed, somehow go back to the sepia-toned world of 1950's farming!

From that moment, I began to look around my world more carefully and clearly, the same attitude seemed to be pervasive with some people. Yet the future bears little respect for such thinking and in the era of acceleration, drives even faster change.

Think about the context of the quote I use on stage. More than anything, it captures in a nutshell the unease that has led to much of the political turmoil around the world over the last few years. There seemed to be a widespread sentiment that the world of globalization, disruption and technological change was happening too fast and should be stopped dead in its tracks. Make things slow down! Some people, for example, seem to want a robust coal industry to come back, just like it was in the 'olden days,' however renewable energy continues its relentless march forward.

Years later, I would look back at this talk and experience as a harbinger of what transpired with the massive election upheaval of 2016, and a portion of the electorate that seemed to vote for a pause button, a return to the past, and a world that would simply stop in its track and keep everything the way it was.

From that point on, I determined that a key part of my stage message would involve the issue of our personal attitude towards the future.

Mindset matters!

If this is the way you react to new technologies and new ways of working, then you are making it almost certain that you'll battle progress — and as soon as you do, you'll be setting yourself back.

The thing is, the future has always led to change and unless you align yourself and turn that change into an opportunity, you are impacted in a negative way. The inevitability of trends means that change will continue to unfold and in an era of acceleration, will have a greater and faster impact than ever before.

Tomorrow

*"Reinvent yourself faster because it will be tomorrow
before you know it!"*

othing lasts forever and today, the new rule of business is that nothing can last beyond a few months! With that, the ability to respond quickly to change is becoming a corner-stone of opportunity.

Products don't last as long as they used to. We replace our cell phones at a furious pace and as products become smart, connected and technology driven, we will come to replace them at the same pace.

Business models don't have any longevity. As soon as you think you have it figured out, some upstart comes along and changes the dynamics within the industry.

The Story Behind the Picture

I know that I worked on this photo when I was on an international flight, somewhere over Iceland. I was heading to Dubai from my home in North America. I was on my way to speak at the World Government Summit. I decided that I better have my morning quote ready to go when I landed, but was pretty confused at that point as to what time it was. It was either 11:30PM EST in Toronto, where I had just left, or 8:30AM Thursday in Dubai, which is where I would land in another 9 hours.

Sometimes, the context of the moment just provides you the inspiration for a quote and an idea!

As soon as you have a great new social media driven marketing strategy, your competition will do something better.

As soon as you get the right structure in place to deal with fast change, you'll find that it isn't adequate to help you cope with the speed of change.

Do you get the point? All of this means that you need to reinvent your company faster than ever before — the products you sell, the skills that you have, the structure you exist by, the strategy you pursue.

Companies that survive thrive in this modern day whirlwind by reinventing themselves at a pace that has gone from fast to furious. Apple set the pace over a decade ago, when it was willing to toss out an entire iPod Nano product line worth billions of dollars of revenue, replacing it with a newer, up-to-date product known as a smartphone. They are now in a situation in which they reinvent so quickly that it is estimated that at one point, 60% of their revenue comes from products that didn't exist 4 years ago.

How could a company choose to cannibalize its own product revenue? Because it recognizes the critical importance of constant reinvention.

I recently spoke at a leadership meeting for a global organization, where the CEO spoke of a future in which the company's success would come from what he called "chameleon revenue" — the sales derived from entirely new product lines. The chart he presented said it all: the organization's future consisted of a steady decrease in baseline revenue and accelerating revenue streams from markets it currently did not participate in.

This will become the norm for most organizations. The ability to rapidly enter and exit markets will define future success. The ability to sustain multiple, short-term product lifecycles, each perhaps no more than 36 to 48 months long, will be a critical success factor. Agility at discovering, producing and capitalizing

on new revenue sources will be a fundamental necessity. In other words, your ability to change your spots and your colour on a dime will be the key driver for your potential.

Everything will be continually different, and you can't hope to get by on the same ideas, skills, methods, concepts and actions that worked for you in the past — you need to continually challenge yourself to do things that are new.

You need to be in a state of constant reinvention!

Simplicity!

"Simplicity is the new complexity!"

We live in the world of the Google search box and the iPhone touch screen. We have little patience for anything that takes more than a moment to figure out. This has implications for everything we do, from how we consume information, to how we learn, to how we exercise!

I often raise the point on stage that today's consumer has little patience, a zero-second attention span and a desire to do things in a rush. The challenge for my clients— many Fortune 500 organizations — is that their customer facing systems need to talk to big, complex, vast back end systems. The result is a series of screens that are complex to navigate, difficult to understand and impossible to finish.

The Story Behind the Picture

This was from a keynote in Chicago for a conference in the ERP (Enterprise Resource Planning) industry. This is the massive software system behind the scenes which many large organizations use to manage all of their affairs from manufacturing to supply chain management, customer ordering to order tracking.

At this particular point in the keynote, I was on the first of 3 slides: the simple Google search box, followed by an iPhone touch screen. I then put up a typical corporate customer facing form — full of all kinds of boxes that you need to fill out. The customer is looking for simplicity yet is faced with stunning complexity.

The challenge for these big organizations is that trying to make these complex systems very easy to use and interact with is a tremendous challenge — and hence, they are today's new complexity.

Have you ever tried to apply for a loan or mortgage online? Every box that you don't finish seems to scream at you!

The same attitude bleeds into our lives off-screen. If we are given instructions on how to do something, it better be fast and straightforward. If we ask a stranger for directions, we'll barely take the time to get past the second step. If we've got a gym routine explained to us, well.....

In an era where attention spans are challenged, simplicity is the response!

Next Opportunity

"A life in a shambles is really just in transition to the next opportunity!"

I think if I ever retire, I will get into the role of a career counsellor!

In the last few days, I've had another close friend with a sudden, unexpected and nerve wracking change in his job circumstances. My job is now to help him by moving his focus from challenge to opportunity.

That's what I do on stage all over the world. I'm regularly encouraging people to take on the challenge of the negativity of business model disruption and turn it into opportunity through innovative thinking.

The Story Behind the Picture

I'm at an HR conference speaking about the future of skills, jobs, careers and opportunities. I'm observing that existing knowledge is going out of date faster than ever before, while new knowledge appears at a furious pace.

The impact? The disappearance of existing jobs at the same time that new ones appear and essentially, a lot of personal career upheaval!

So it's only natural that I help out a good buddy by doing the same thing!

Here's a fact: it's when you become comfortable that bad fortune decides to slam you in the head and batter you about! It's what you do with it that matters.

When bad things happen to good people — what's done is done. It's time to move on, to put effort into positioning yourself for the next opportunity, rather than focusing on the last one.

A shift in attitude is a critical part of the process. It's really like the seven stages of grief, I've got to move him quickly beyond the shock and anger stage into acceptance! Once you accept the finality of your powerlessness over your situation, you can begin to make the necessary changes and put in the proper effort to move to the next stage!

What is that next stage? Capturing the full range of the awesomeness of the skills, capabilities and enthusiasm he has already brought to his resume so far! Making his skills and capabilities shine in such a way that people will be clamouring for his services, not the other way around!

Once you move from being a hunter to someone who is being hunted, you've made the necessary shift!

Throughout your life, there are moments where you must accept the fact that what is done is done - you can't fix the past. You can only change the future.

There is only what you decide to do today to prepare for your new reality of tomorrow!

Tomorrow's Certainty

"Today's impossibility?
It's tomorrow's certainty"

I've recently been using the phrase "era of acceleration" quite a bit to explain to my audiences that things are speeding up, everything is becoming faster, velocity increases are the new normal.

The result? Anything that is impossible today will likely be a reality tomorrow. No idea is too big; no goal too small; no initiative is too timid. It's what you will do with that reality that matters!

Be prepared for people to push back on your ideas. Get ready for some laughter and hoots of derision when you talk about your goal.

The Story Behind the Picture

It came to me as soon as I saw one of the boldest moves by Space-X — landing rocket launchers, upright, on a ship, in the ocean! What a time to be alive!

You can't have a forward thinking mind and not have a tear come to your eye when you watch @SpaceX land 3 rocket boosters after launch.

You can bet that when the concept was first raised years ago, someone said "that's the dumbest idea I've ever heard." And yet, here we are!

Space travel? Rockets?

"The dumbest idea I ever heard!" That's what everyone told Robert Goddard, one of the fathers of modern rocketry (the other being the brilliant Russian rocket pioneer Konstantin Tsiolkovsky.)

All kinds of people told Robert Goddard that his idea of a moon rocket was absolute lunacy.

Just as some might have told Elon Musk and the folks at SpaceX that their idea for an upright landing was crazy.

Get this — even the New York Times predicted we'd never land on the moon! They later apologized after Apollo 11.

Be bold in your thinking, clear in your objectives and big in your ideas. Ignore those who would tell you it can't be done.

Their minds are far too small to comprehend your potential achievements!

Seize The Opportunity!

"Today you have the chance to start to live the best life you will ever live! Will you seize the opportunity?"

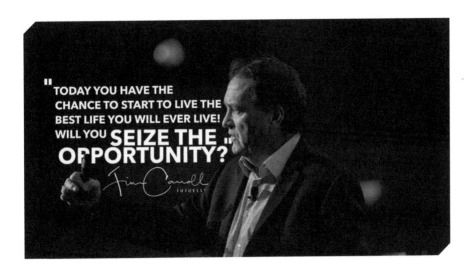

How many times do you sit back and say to yourself, "if I had only done things differently!"

Yet, when have you actually done things differently? Did you ever seize the opportunity when it was right in front of you?

Every morning, you face a conscious decision — will you make today a great day or just another marginal day in a string of marginal days?

Will you work hard to pursue your passion and purpose, or will you just go through the motions?

The Story Behind the Picture

These daily motivational quotes have become my morning mantra, my method of starting the day out right in a proper, great frame of mind.

They began as a brief tool of inspiration after a difficult stage in my life. I'd start my day with coffee, think about the day ahead and spend my time thinking of some sort of observation that would help to make my forthcoming day a personal success.

Within a week, I began to wake in the morning, looking forward to this morning moment of inspirational thinking; I would be immersed in my motivation; inspired by my opportunity!

The quotes began to take on a life of their own. As I wrap up completion of this book I am now close to 1,000 of these daily motivations. I don't intend on slowing it down.

Because each and every day, I make a conscious decision to try to live the best life that I can live.

Thank you for reading.

Will you do the things you should be doing that you know are better for you, or will you abandon your potential success to the old, bad habits of yesterday?

I'm a big fan of starting each day with conscious purpose, with a goal and with a bit of reflection on the things I will do that day to make the day a better day.

I exchanged these thoughts through the weekend with a good friend who is struggling with his ability to keep things in check. Emails were flying back and forth as I shared my relentless optimism with him as a pathway for opportunity.

I was out hiking while doing so, and at one point, made the comment found in today's quote with him as being reflective of my own state of mind.

And it is. Each morning, I start out knowing that it's in me to make it a great day — and so I'll start out with that goal in mind.

Today, start to live the first day of the best days of the rest of your life!

You can learn more about Jim on his web site:

https://jimcarroll.com

Follow and connect with Jim on various online networks:

Twitter: @jimcarroll   Instagram: futuristjimcarroll

Facebook: futuristjimcarroll   Flickr: futurist-jimcarroll

LinkedIn: https://www.linkedin.com/in/carrolljim

You will find a daily inspirational observation, much as you found in this book, on all of these social networks as well as at:

https://inspiration.jimcarroll.com

About The Author

Jim Carroll is the world's leading futurist, trends and innovation expert, with a massive global Blue Chip client list. Over the last 25 years, Jim has shared his insight from the stage with over 2 million people as a keynote speaker, speaking on topics relating to the future of energy and transportation, retail trends and consumer behaviour, the future of healthcare and agriculture.

Jim's clients include NASA, Disney, the World Bank, Mercedes Benz, the PGA, and over a thousand more.

His global client list gives him a front row seat to the high velocity change that is occurring as disruption comes to take hold of every industry and every organization.

With that insight and the customized research that he undertakes for every engagement, he helps to transform growth-oriented organizations into high-velocity innovation heroes!

CPSIA information can be obtained
at www.ICGtesting.com
Printed in the USA
BVHW022345130220
572250BV00004BA/21

9 780973 655476